THREE
LEAVES,
THREE
ROOTS

THREE LEAVES, THREE ROOTS

POEMS ON THE HAITI–CONGO STORY

■ ■ ■ ■ ■ ■ ■ ■ ■

DANIELLE LEGROS GEORGES

RAISED VOICES

BEACON PRESS, BOSTON

BEACON PRESS
Boston, Massachusetts
www.beacon.org

Beacon Press books
are published under the auspices of
the Unitarian Universalist Association of Congregations.

28 27 26 25   8 7 6 5 4 3 2 1

This book is printed on acid-free paper that meets the uncoated paper
ANSI/NISO specifications for permanence as revised in 1992.

Text design and composition by Kim Arney

Raised Voices is a poetry series established in 2021 to raise marginalized
voices and perspectives, to publish poems that affirm progressive values and
are accessible to a wide readership, and to celebrate poetry's ability
to access truth in a way that no other form can.

*Library of Congress Cataloguing-in-Publication
Data is available for this title.*
Paperback ISBN: 978-0-8070-2048-7
E-book ISBN: 978-0-8070-2049-4

TWA FEY

Twa fey, twa rasin, O
Jete bliye, ranmase sonje

Mwen gen basin mwen
Twa fey tonbe ladann

Jete bliye, ranmase sonje . . .

■ ■ ■

THREE LEAVES

Three leaves, three roots, O
Cast them off and forget, reclaim them and remember

I have my basin here
Three leaves fall into it

Cast them off and forget, reclaim them and remember . . .

—*traditional Haitian song*

CONTENTS

INTRODUCTION

During the 1960s and 1970s, in the wake of the Democratic Republic of the Congo's independence from Belgium, hundreds of young Haitian professionals answered a joint call from the new country and the United Nations to move there and contribute their skills. As Haiti's unstable political climate left them little opportunity to practice in their fields in their home country, and with growing numbers facing persecution under the dictatorship of François Duvalier, most saw the fellow Black francophone nation's call for French-speaking educators—as well as doctors, engineers, lawyers, and other professionals—as an opportunity to escape repression and launch their careers. By the mid-'60s, Haitians represented a large number of the Congo's foreign experts.

A great deal has been written about Haiti's general history, particularly its extraordinary 1804 revolution, which has served as a model for liberation struggles in the United States, Latin America, and Africa. Scholars have also paid careful attention to the Haiti of the 1950s through the 1980s, in particular to what anthropologist Michel-Rolph Trouillot calls "the longest dictatorial sequence in the history of that country." Until recently, however, very little has been written about this pioneer group of Haitians in the Congo.

This book is meant as an artistic introduction to this little-known Black transnational narrative—what I call the Haiti-Congo story. It is a story that has implications for the study of twentieth-century Black transnational collaborations and contributions to make in the areas of postcolonial studies, cross-border intellectual histories, Caribbean migration, Haitian transnationalism and identity, the roles of governments and NGOs, the political and economic dimensions of geographic displacement in general, and the negotiations of race, gender, and class by migrant workers.

For me, the Haiti-Congo story is also personal: it is the story of my parents, Edmonde Legros and Rodney Georges, who had begun professional lives in Haiti—my mother as a secondary school teacher and my father as an engineer and architect—shortly before they moved to the Congo in 1965. It is also the story of their dear friends and colleagues. It begins for me in the 1970s, growing up in Boston and seeing my mother and her friends in their skirts made from fabric bought in the Congo, with hearing them drop Congolese Lingala terms into their Creole and French conversations. It is the tale of my father, for whom Sunday afternoons entailed playing Congolese records, whereupon much shaking of the tail feather could be seen. It is the story of heated political debates, which is the Haitian way, among friends and family in my childhood living room. These debates took on, obliquely or directly, Pan-Africanism, a liberated Haiti, the Civil Rights Movement in the United States, Black Power, and Latin American nationalisms.

The evidence of my family's time in the Congo was everywhere in our home—in the form of paintings, mementos, an impossibly big gold ring bearing the profile of Nefertiti that belonged to my mother. (Bequeathed to me, I now don it when needing extra power to deal with oppressive structures or troublesome individuals). Yet it did not occur to me to think of that time as a narrative—much less an area of historical study or literary investigation—until the early 2000s, when I began to read and translate a cache of letters from my parents to my paternal grandmother, along with documents she had saved from their time there. These helped reveal my parents to me in ways I'd never before known or understood them. Their everyday concerns, the broad structures they were negotiating, the money they were sending back home to Haiti, the care for their children and family members, their complaints, their travels—all came into sharp focus. Moreover, that they were not alone in these experiences, and that they belonged to a close-knit group of Haitians who would later lay the groundwork for Boston's current Haitian community (the largest in the United States after Miami and New York) made me understand that *theirs* and *there* was a story to be told.

By the time I began to research the Haiti-Congo narrative, the Congo participants were getting on in years, and some had died (my own father had passed years earlier). I sought to identify and interview as many participants as time permitted. I found our exchanges profoundly fruitful, grounded in the generosity of my interlocutors as we explored questions of micro and macro history—and the reverberations of this history today.

The narratives of the Haitian men often began in political contexts. The narratives of the Haitian women added texture to the story. In addition to comments on geopolitics, the women spoke of their domestic spaces and of their interactions with neighbors, door-to-door Congolese market women, their colleagues, and, in some cases, their students.

The men were, generally, the first in their families to be offered jobs in the Congo, usually by the United Nations Educational, Scientific, and Cultural Organization (UNESCO). After the men arrived in Africa, women then secured jobs from UNESCO and such organizations as the Salvation Army. Several women recalled to me the challenges of traveling from the

Americas to Africa, alone or with children, to join their husbands and partners in the Congo. Several women arrived in the Congo to find their men in ill health or malnourished and set about nursing them back to health. The women spoke of collaborating to procure food in markets when food was scarce and—when circumstances were easier—of the popular Portuguese *pregos* sandwiches and Primus beer in cafés. They discussed supporting one another's children, some of whom were born in the Congo. Their letters to relatives in Haiti addressed the details of home-making in the new country. The letters of both Haitian women and men referenced the remittances they were sending to Haiti to support their relatives there.

In the Congo, the young Haitians made their way to towns and rural areas or bush across the vast republic, a country with a population more than six times that of Haiti. They were six thousand miles away from home. Some would work in Kinshasa (formerly Léopoldville), others at sites in the country's interior, such as Lodja and Kisangani (formerly Stanleyville). Some found themselves on the eastern border in Butembo, Goma, Bukavu, and Kalemi (Albertville), or in the western towns of Kikwit, Tshikapa, Bandundu (Banningville), and Kenge. Haitians also traveled to and lived in the southern cities of Kananga (Luluabourg) and Lubumbashi (Elisabethville), and in the eastern cities of Kitona, Matadi, and Boma, not far from the Atlantic coast.

They encountered cultures, dynamics, and phenomena that were both familiar and new. Among these was a new colonialism not known to them in Haiti. The Belgian Congo had been established in 1908 for the extraction and plunder of the territory's resources, including rubber, cobalt, diamonds, copper, uranium, and gold. The Haitians were unaccustomed to the apartheid they saw in the major cities of the Congo. The Congolese capital of Léopoldville/Kinshasa, for example, contained a "white" city center, in which the remaining Europeans lived, and a "black" periphery, or *cité*, a ghetto that had been created earlier for the Congolese by Europeans. Under Belgian colonial rule, and for as long as Belgians remained and wielded some power in the postcolonial capital, most Congolese were discouraged or kept from circulating in the white section after dark, forbidden from stores and public accommodations. Also, the idea and perception of class, which governed a great deal of Haitian urban society—particularly the small black middle class from which the majority of the émigrés came—did not operate as pervasively with the Congolese. In Congolese social realities, ethnic group affiliations were central to one's identity. In addition, poverty in the Congolese urban centers was not necessarily accompanied by the monolingualism and illiteracy emblematic of the Haitian urban poor, who highly valued formal education but did not have widespread access to it. Almost all Haitians spoke Creole, but only a minority had access to formal education and thus also spoke French. Every Congo émigré came from this francophone minority. Francophonie thus broadcasted an instant class signal for Haitians. Not so for the Congolese, in a nation in which more than two hundred languages were spoken. Whereas, in Haiti, French served to separate the classes, in Congo it served as a unifying language, one that facilitated communication among the Congolese, the Haitians, the Belgians, and others.

Many participants would stay in the Congo fewer than ten years. A number would remain well into the 1980s, and some are still living there. Numerous participants spoke of the lifelong friendships forged with one another. They also underscored their appreciation for their Congolese colleagues and students, and for Congolese culture(s). Despite cultural differences between the Haitians and Congolese, friendships, collaborations, and families emerged between them as a result of the work they did together.

Several participants said they developed a heightened political consciousness as a result of their Congo experiences. Afterwards, they were better able to connect seemingly disparate progressive struggles within and beyond the African diaspora and to identify challenges to democratic movements.

Among Haiti's narratives are two familiar and persistent ones that disproportionately shape outside perceptions of the nation: first, Haiti's significant 1804 revolution as the source of inspiration for antislavery, anti-imperial, freedom-seeking peoples the world over; second, Haiti considered the poorest nation in the Western Hemisphere, a perpetual site of need. These tropes locate Haiti in the centuries-old past on the one hand and outside of time on the other. Between these narratives runs the thread of a third unremitting one: that of an unspoken and frightening darkness, not disconnected to the first two and not unlike that attached to representations of Africa and Africans.

Not often mentioned in the discourse about Haiti are its universities, its long traditions of higher education, its training of students in law, education, medicine, economics, pharmacy, engineering, urban planning, literature, agriculture, accounting and finance, management and administration, and environmental studies. Its specialists and pioneers have tended to be viewed as exceptional and not as emerging from (and responding to) structures extant in Haiti.

The Haiti-Congo story presents us with a community of Haitians who articulate an awareness of themselves in time. They are a group who exercised agency in greatly constrained circumstances—a group who benefited from Haitian institutions and pushed against their compromise, who operated through the gears of UNESCO and the Congolese government. Most were deeply sympathetic to the cause of Congolese independence and to the Congolese they worked with, even as they composed part of the UN's elite multinational working corps, which some argue ultimately supported Western interests in the Congo. They also represented a loss of human capital for Haiti—at a moment when perhaps Haiti needed them most. At the same time, like many diasporic Haitians, they economically supported loved ones and relatives in Haiti with ongoing remittances. They were Black and mixed-race and privileged, and in many cases cosmopolitan and deeply committed to their country of origin. Most importantly for our purposes, they were willing to write—however difficult or complicated—their individual narratives, a collective story of collaboration, and a new Haitian transatlantic narrative.

This book's title draws from "Twa Fey," a song well known in Haitian popular culture. It is meant to evoke the themes of memory and remembrance; of what we keep, what we remember, what we cast off, what we forget, what we lose. It is also tied to the idea of resistance, connected to the Haitian proverb *The day the leaf falls in the water is not the day it rots*. In other words: you may fall, but you will not perish. A proverb for the underdog. A proverb for a country that has stumbled but has not perished.

CONGO—1960s

BECAUSE

they had founded a country, rose
to claim their state, made Blackness
the mouth of freedom . . .

WHITES IN CONGO FLEE BY FERRY

New York Times, July 9, 1960: "Reports of rape and murder by drunken African troops threw whites into panic in Leopoldville today and sent men, women and children fleeing in terror for safety."

To *flee*. To *feel*. Distance signified by the order of consonants. To be aware. Of someone. Of some thing. Through touch. Through being touched. To sense *flame*. To meet its embers,

the matter that remains after, or sometimes precedes, *a fire*. To run from a place, site of danger (when you are the danger). To scurry aboard the ferry, suitcases in hand. To have no words for this.

IN THIS POEM, DO NOT USE THE WORD REVOLUTION

use instead a slow swelling of light that begins at a
beginning when the scar-giver forges the scar and forgets,
and the bearer remembers indelibly the mark on the body,
recalls how a mark can be made on a body. in the ear a clear
consciousness whispered. use instead *reply* because peace
is a place free of trouble: a blue firmament, a gold sun that
reaches the skin. use instead the equalization of all suns, the
standing next to, the standing for, rotation, and the equi-
librium of stars: objects held together by their own gravity.
gravity is the flame of dissonance, is the mind honed with
the vision of its unity. grave is the fist raised of the body.

HANDS ARE A MATTER,

brown as the bark of wild rubber trees
tapped, latex dripping

like milk. Rubber. A colony is a good
mother, a pearl

reflecting light from surface, drawn
of internal glow—irritation

become luster, a term flushed of origin.
Quota is another word driving

the rising magnitude. A drain toward
the metropole.

Belgium is to Congo as mouth is to hand.
As wealth is to soil.

A scandal hangs in history. It trickles,
rubber from the trees.

Incisions in the bark. Smooth growl
of the rainforest.

The many hands required of the harvest.
And when the rubber does

not come? The hands themselves.
Piles offered

to the overlord's gluttonous gods.
Black hands.

The daughter of the chief's hand.
The children of the pauper's hands.

COBALT

Word the other and make the world.

Name the land *Maiden. Mother*.

Mineral field.

Blue as the cobalt contained in my hand.

Blue as a sky full of satellites.

Radio waves sent

Down.

Dark as the mine.

Dark as a pithead of minerals-making-possible.

Dark as the skin

Of the collier.

White as the resource-

War.

White as a colonization.

Green as the jungle.

Green as the top of the earth.

Massive lung. Human

Lung.

Called is the jewel

Of the earth:

Tantalum from coltan.

Diamond. Gleaming.

Culled is the copper. Orange glow.

Culled the cobalt.

Culled the wrist's

Gold.

MY BELOVED COMPANION,

I write you these words not knowing whether you will receive them,
when you will receive them, and whether I will still be alive when

you read them: opening, the letter knows itself to be a vision :
a key proper to the dark lock and behind the door : a plane

of light muted as a savannah's revelation of a woman walking
fringed by children: hers : his : a nation's : the writer formed

by the ink of a self-determination, a broader promise, *what we*
wanted for our country — its right to an honorable life, to perfect

dignity, to independence with no restrictions : he knows his wife
will not read the letter: she will hear it read : he knows, reader,

that you will know he speaks to you : *What else can I say?* he writes.
It is not my person that is important. What is important is the Congo

. . . people whose independence has been turned into a cage, with people
looking at us from outside the bars he says, through bars :

outside : in : how his faith will remain unshakable :
how *We are not alone.*

A REPLY OF PAULINE OPANGO LUMUMBA

To walk bare-breasted
In protest how the crowds
Part

How the fist-sized heart
Starts and stays
With a knack

Of its own seasons
Its own seizures
Grief

Is the public act
Of a woman open
As a dare

Do not hold me
Léopoldville
Site

Of such spillage
Such savage
Extraction

Site of my husband's
Irretrievable
Frame

LE CONGO, C'EST MOI

And yet my congo is there
In this hydrolysis, this decomposition and transformation.

The right formula will
do it, antidotal, anti-venom. *Five and two make seven the golden*

number and the end
of the world's troubles, though the waters remain disturbed,

fluent in the alkaline
language of martyr's blood, filling with iron the tributaries

through dams
through captured flows nonetheless bearing above the algae

that very name
serving as key to every open mouth to the broad dazzle of the coral.

* * *

Le Congo, c'est moi
write savior and poet, write both hands of one body, say

lingala, swahili,
kituba, tshiluba, mashi, mongo, kilega, tetela, chokwe,

say budza, ngbandi,
lendu, mangbetu, yombe, nande, ngbaka, zande, lugbara,

say komo, say
kinyarwanda and indubil: *I place your name beneath a flower.*

Beneath what flower?
On what stone? In which hand? In what night?

CUBA—1950s

BECAUSE

A world split in two
Hemispheres

Will not please the new-
World gods.

FIDEL WEARS NO HAT

You are walking through Central Park, New York.
You have what is called swagger, face cocked.

The buildings around you glow, the air around
you moves, a taxi whizzes by. Silent

October. The leaves prepare a riot.
Your suit and vest as serious

as a set of law books. You are a man
prepared to do things with your bare hands.

A tempest brews over uncut fields. Your father's
green cane. You have come to make a deal

with the future, with a Mexican mountain range,
with the harbor waters of Tuxpan, 1956.

Right now, you'll take all the Yankee
dollars you can get. This evening

you'll have the Hotel Palm Garden Hall,
the well-dressed exiles by their beautiful

collars, express in no uncertain terms:
Batista must go. The greenbacks will float

from pockets and purses. They'll pile high
on the banquet table. You will make it rain.

Isla de Pinos, marzo 22 de 1955

ESTIMADA AMIGA,

*. . . The inscription on your card was so beautifully written
that I have my hopes set on the pleasure of receiving a letter
from you soon. The only variant, I hope, will be that you use
"tu" instead of "usted." Could this be too much to hope for?*

> writes Fidel reeling in María Laborde who will
> bear him a son. She wants to be reeled in. She will
> be. He's about to be freed. His captors don't know
> he will be their greatest regret. How he will stretch
> from the Isla de Pinos like a beautiful tree, like
> the knotting of roots, like a gnarling.

*Today I will be brief. Write me in the same way as if I, more
courteous and well-mannered, had long ago answered your two
letters, thus carrying on a long correspondence . . .*

HAITI—1960s

BECAUSE

they had named themselves
   in the third version of the rising
                world

because they had
       uttered
          freedom ages ago

BECAUSE

every freedom break
must wreck
the past

INSTRUCTIONS IN TIMES OF EMERGENCY

Turn the radio low but listen.
A slow rustle. (A dictator.)

Do not turn (though some
Turn) against

A neighbor. Do not look
A beached

And bloated body in its face.
Do not plead

To God. Witness
The executions.

Your human self, keep it
Alive. A type

Of flame. Your lizard self,
Your toughest skin,

Wear it. Shut your door
Against the night.

Keep your door shut
Against the creeping

Night.

WHEN A BOOK IS A SENTENCE

it will lie stone-faced under a bed,
still as a snake.

It will curl in a cabinet holding
a life in its rattle.

It will stretch a memorandum
of understanding

between the reader and her
rebellion.

When a book is a sentence
it freezes when it's found.

It may not know what
it was doing

there in your house, glowing
like a bright red moon.

FRANÇOIS DUVALIER, COUNTRY DOCTOR

Infections of the skin and bone.
Berry-red sores on the youngest

Ones. Peasants say *pitit se richès
Malere*. Did he not save yours

When disease came cloaked to eat
Them? Did he not hold

Their hands in this hard-hearted
Heat, a gentle uncle?

The peasants say *children are
The wealth of the poor*,

The countryside's gold, small
Gods of happiness,

Alive to ensure the approaching
Dawn. Did they not flourish

Like the coffee, like the corn
Sending taproot down,

Pushing first leaves up
Into the air?

Did they not suit
His harvest?

FRANÇOIS DUVALIER, LIVING GOD

To be a living god. To occupy the axis
of two planes of existence.
Spirit. Incarnate.

To retrieve from the abysmal waters,
abode of the dead. The deep call
to deep.

To run the realm of rebellious spirits,
great as the third birth,
black

as the crushed hibiscus flower
in the sun's ultra
glare.

To pluck the cotton pieces for
the nostrils from the *cruche*
of cotton.

To soak in alcohol the scent
of your concerns,
the symbols

of your urgencies. To jail
your tongue. To nail
your savior

once again to his cross. To
don the finest tall hat,
the whitest gloves.

SIMONE DUVALIER

Made of mud and expensive clay,
I am given away.

I train. I live. I nurse,
Prim in white

As a loaded bride. Writer's child,
Heir of his maid,

Whose color you know. My mother,
Who wants so much

For me, who lets me go. And there,
We know, he is,

Clean in white coat and necklace
Of a stethoscope.

Pulse contained as a metronome. Music
Of my heart. Music

Of my mind pulsing *Yes*. Black man.
Peerless sheen, eye

-Glass frames. The pull of his gaze.
The pull of my gaze.

We will make three girls. We will
Make the boy-king

Like a nineteenth-century dauphin
In a *royaume* of crossroads

Where all maps meet the contracts
Of flesh. Where alignments

Of stars by ordained calculation
Connect small and great

Gods. In the courtyards of lead-white
Butterflies.

With the eating of cake. If hunger
Makes me,

What also makes me is a dream:
My own self,

Formidable. Fixed like a pocket
On a jacket.

Like a *paquet d'affaires*. Like
The key to the lock

To the room of gunpowder.
Of gold. I'm as neat

As a black dress with ribbons.
I'm a cinched waist,

Imperious as shoulder pads.
Wife and mother

Of dictators. A woman who
Has everything

To say, and will find a way
To say it.

CROSSINGS—1960s

BECAUSE

freedom does not die easily

because it rides the black waves

DIASPORA

Diaspora is a word. Diaspora is a non-wish,
A sour dance. A heavy drum.

Is a wandering in the utter until something
Opens up: Seas. Desert.

Is a dune to confound your place in the caravan.
Over which the moon appears

A knife of narrow white.

DIASPORA

Diaspora is a raining down.
Is a green remittance.

Is a holding. Down. A floating.
Kin. The absinthe of sea

Speaking beneath.

WHAT IS WATER?

What is water but rain but cloud but river but ocean
but ice but tear.

What is tear but torn what is worn as skin as in as out
as out.

Exodus. I am trying to tell a tale that shifts like a gale
that hurricanes

casting a line that buckles in wind that is reborn a kite
a wing. I am

Far from the planes & suitcases, passports & degrees,
from the heat

from the cluster of Haitians descending,
raining down.

BECAUSE

empires
sever.

Because
diasporas

disrupt

empires.

Fischbach, 1 February 1966

I PRAY THE UNITED NATIONS BUREAU WILL FORWARD THIS CARD TO MY BROTHER RODNEY GEORGES WHO IS CURRENTLY IN THE CONGO, WHOSE ADDRESS I DON'T KNOW

Dear Brother,

Our mother made me aware that you have been in the Congo since October 1965. She complains of no word from you.

Already 7 years have passed since we parted. Time has stopped for me. I'm working as an engineer at Dornier where the first vertical transport plane is being built.

I am the only foreigner, not to mention the only Black man here . . .

Your brother,

Gérard

Léopoldville, 17 February 1966

LETTER FROM LÉO

Dear Mother,

      I imagine how much you've suffered

                      with no word from me

for three months.

                  I suffered

knowing   what you could have feared.

                  I went

—no—was sent

    to a remote province.

The local authorities there

                  did everything they could

                    to make

our lives miserable.

                  They did not like Haitians.

They cut

    our communication with the exterior.

Our letters
        were blocked.

We were, in effect, prisoners.

                        I was finally able to get out

        of that cursed place.

If everything

works out, I'll stay in Léo.

If Léo gives us trouble,

        I'll go to Germany

to look for work

        and study.

If this doesn't work

        I will go

        to the UNITED STATES.
Otherwise,

        I will return home.

Dear mother

        my account has not been updated

I can send you nothing right now.

      Send me Gérard's address in Germany.

          Cable it as soon as you can.

I wrote Serge, you, and Edouard,

      each two letters from Inongo. They were,

      no doubt, confiscated in Inongo.

Now I am at the address above.

      While waiting for your news,

receive Dear Mother,

    the affection and kisses of your son

      who has never stopped thinking of you.

Rodney

THE REASONS OF JACQUELINE ROMAIN

Ma chère, I'll tell you this,
I'm a woman who makes up her own mind.

Before I left Haiti, what was I
Thinking? Of my freedom, naturally.

Of René too, but I didn't say this
Or even make it word in my mind's mouth.

The heart drums—and the heart
Is one way to keep time, to write one's

Own lines. I carved a way. I left
Port-au-Prince. I flew to Paris. I did what

I had to do. Four days stuck in a
Hotel room. The cold. I found a friend who

Had a friend. (You have to know
people to make things move, papers, what

Needs agreeing to.) And without much
delay, there I was on a flight to Kinshasa,

En route to everything I knew,
And everything I did not know.

THE REASONS OF RIGOBERT CARTY

Before I left

    Haiti for Congo

I confess I had

    exotic ideas

(so bereft was I of clear

knowledge:

    vast forests

      wild beasts

    strange verdure

      danger) .

I know now.

    But the first news

from Inongo

    magnified my impression:

A python

    with a cow's

        bulk in it.

Digestion to take three

    months, the mammal

melting

    in a tomb of cold blood.

But that was the least

    of my concerns.

I had cast a ballot.

    I had checked:

    François Duvalier,

pushed in

    the greatest

    pressure.

François Duvalier,

head

    and body growing long

tail stretching

    hill to gulley

        to cities.

I was so sickened

    I vowed to leave

my country

—*my own country*—

    as soon as I could.

I couldn't stomach

    the treason.

These

    are my reasons.

Inongo, 1965

THE LAKE BEHIND YOU

The fronds you peer from
far-flung

make shadows of the ferns
knee-deep

you are photographed green
in them

unfurling shrines beneath
a sanctuary

of trees equatorially grown
so tall

so fed by the lake nearby
water of the earth

water of the air of Inongo.
A hot hell

you call this place. Such
humidity

such blankness to Black
foreigners like

you. So many useless
letters posted

never to not arrive. But
one does, saying

nothing of Inongo's
milk-blue sky.

Nothing of the lake behind
you, full of crocodiles.

THYSVILLE, 1966

On the back of a black and white
photograph, my father writes
my mother *Thysville,*

20 Fevrier 1966. To her he dedicates
himself and the two girls above
whom he stands,

a hand on a shoulder of each. *Gesi*
et Gema t'embrassent bien fort
he notes, eyes

frozen forward, cigarette between
his lips, handsome as a god
bearing documents

from the firmament to the gravel.
In the pocket of his white shirt,
a black notebook slender

as a new passport. In white dresses
Gesi and Gema cable the care
and discomfort

of cultivated children. If we take
the order of my father's
reference, read left

to right, Gesi, the smallest, is first,
thumb-in-mouth, peering
into the distance.

Gema won't be caught so, meeting
with her fierce gaze
the image-maker.

Who is her father? Her mother?
They must be girls of my
father's friends.

Thysville stands this moment,
pigheaded child of a colonial
christening.

Not for much longer.
Gesi, Gema, where are you
in the great world

after Thysville ceased
to be?

HEADWATERS

infants in tow

a plane   an address

in hand   a husband

in a distant   place

how long   how far

how streams of

what is ahead   and what

behind   what   after   .

the books hidden

the mouths sealed

the alarmed

tributaries
_____

a leaf dropped
            in headwaters

of the Congo River

will flow

thousands of kilometers

past rapids   past massive

waterfalls

on slow
          currents

to join the Atlantic Ocean

THE REASONS OF ERTHA ÉLYSÉE AUGUSTE

to ask Ertha Élysée Auguste for her reasons
is to beckon successions of waves. is to
struggle to make this a flow.
a poem. her account.

will not be restrained. because. she will
not be restrained. such a woman.
raised by women. we will not
say poto mitan (middle post
of a temple) (wooden
beam) (outstretched
arms affixed)
(holding
everything (and everyone) up)

we will say/she will say
>I didn't go there to be a housewife. I saw
>myself as someone with a career. I come from
>a family of working women. My grandmother
>was a madan sara. She had a daughter
>recognized by a man she was not married
>to. She would go sell in the area markets,
>the grand marché hebdomadaire, well into
>the North. We were from the Artibonite.
>My mother was a seamstress and tailor, a
>commerçante. I had that tradition of women
>who made their own money, women who
>took care of their own children.

we will say/she will say

That was my vision of my role: an
independent person who collaborated with
her husband, who brought her financial
contribution. My husband held this point
of view too, that we would share the family
duties.

she will say

I was in Zaire from 1966 to 1969.

I left Haiti in September.

she will say

I took a little Boeing 313 to join Karl, flying
over the jungle, the lakes, the rich nature.

By contrast, Haiti's earth was poor. There
was a region I visited with my mother when
I was about ten. In '49 or '50 they decided to
celebrate the 150th anniversary of something
or other, and the government introduced
electricity to the Artibonite Valley. They
switched the courses of rivers and tributaries
to achieve this.

Years later, I returned to that very place. I
saw only dust and cadavers of trees with arms
raised in the air, imploring the sky.

she will say

To join Karl, I took a little Boeing 313, with
the children.

I will interpose *courageous*
          root of the word like a clear blade
          root of the word in the heart
          coeur of the substructure
          thus temperament
          state of mind
          spirit

I will interpose
          silver moon
          golden sun

she will say
          We arrived to an almost-deserted airport.

          When we finally saw Karl, it was a moment
          of great joy. The girls flew to him. He
          wrapped us all in his arms.

she will say
          I was given my own teaching contract, during
          my time in Congo. I had vacations every
          year. Every two years, you could go to Haiti,
          expenses paid. The first year, I took the kids
          back.

          In 1967, we went to Europe, then to the US.

here is a photograph
          at whose center stands Ertha—Philippe in her
          arms, Myriam and Sandra in front of her—
          flanked by Karl, beloved husband. Rome is
          the backdrop. Sunlight bathes them there on

the bright plaza. Sunlight bathes the passers-
by all white, gray, black. Ertha's sheath of a
dress is bright. The photograph is black and
white. All compositional roads lead to her.
She is the anchor of the chevron made by the
faces of her family. She is the beauty-mother-
law student-teacher. She is the woman raised
by women beside her husband, adorned by
their children on the plaza. She is the photo's
center. The photographer saw this. The
photographer knew this.

she will say

I taught at two places. First in Luluabourg, at
the École Normale, French literature, but I
expanded the curriculum to include French-
language literature. I taught World History.
When I arrived, there was only one text, *The
Middle Ages*. I had to order books. I paid for
them myself. I asked for reimbursement.
I had to recite the texts, transcribe them,
write them on the board because we couldn't
photocopy easily.

she will have us see

the students, who were fantastic. I learned a great
deal from them. They were mostly eighteen,
some older. They came from very far away in
the *cité*, many from poor families. There were
two who were engaged, the girl was pregnant.
It was a serious situation, the greatest shame

for their parents. They wanted to have a civil marriage. We spoke to the parents. They eventually got married. I will always remember this.

she will say

I would often stay after class to answer my students' questions. Word got out in the community that I was staying after school. This was a point of criticism among some Haitian colleagues. I was among the few female teachers. *Les gents vont commencer à te critiquer* they told me.

I helped my students with social issues, advice, they called me *mama*.

she will say

I often walked home from school. People said I was too proud to ask for a ride. The truth was more complicated.

NOTES ON THE SCHOOL IN KINSHASA

I had a full class, forty students. In Gonaïves,
at the École des Soeurs, we had twenty at most.

They were so ambitious, wanting to grow.
They sat shoulder to shoulder in that

French school, far from their homes. The
teachers came from all over: some Japanese,

French, some Congolese, some Arabs,
Algerians, Lebanese, Moroccans, a Canadian.

The students showed up even during heavy
rains, dripping like rainforest leaves—unlike

in Haiti. *Why?* Because their houses leaked.
They rushed to school, tracking all kinds

of mud. Those students taught me much
about how to live, how to be in the country.

I was at *their* school. They said *this is what
this means*, and *you must not do this*,

and *you must try that*. They were attentive.
With good questions. They took good notes.

Homework was a challenge. They got home
late. They had no electricity, no light.

MAX MANIGAT IN KENGE

As far as the Congolese population was concerned, I was welcome as a long-lost brother.

I started to learn Kikongo, the main language of the province, to communicate with the population.

Officials of the village and our students also spoke French. The Belgian professors, thinking I was

a different kind of Black, warned me against making Congolese friends. Of course, I had Congolese friends.

THE WORK

We taught in the grammar and high schools
across the country—in cities and villages,

under such new skies. We taught according
to what we knew—(& what we thought

we knew) across fields—*français, histoire,
mathematiques, physique et chimie,* more

lessons of the Western texts, the blue flames
of our yearnings and African affinities.

We heated theory in beakers of fresh labs,
held praxis up to light. How eagerly

we arrived, clean as anything, sweating
in our proper clothes

our contracts signed

= G.B/JA. =
-REPUBLIQUE DEMOCRATIQUE DU CONGO.-
GOUVERNEMENT CENTRAL
MINISTÈRE DE L'ÉDUCATION NATIONALE.
-=-=-=-=-=-=-=-=-=-=-=-=-=-=-=
-ADMINISTRATION GENERALE.-
-=-=-=-=-=
1ère Direction
3ème Section.-

our contracts sealed with purple stamps of state
approval: round, and dark as suns dipped in

coagulating ink, bordered by such whims of Belgian
roots that blew up in gusts. We taught in the belly

of a newborn nation, mewling and ancient, green
with so much. Call it flush. We thought like so many

now is the liberation in practice and belief, now
the righteous struggle. We walked to school. Our

students walked too. They sang *we shall show the world*
what the Black man can do when working in liberty and

we shall make the Congo the pride of Africa.
They were proud. We were proud.

Kinshasa, 1967

UNANNOUNCED EVALUATION

I created a course on the Spice Route

       Probing the influence of the Arabs, and slavery.

I put up lots of notes on the board

       During one class. The students were with me.

The Director ambled in. I carried on.

       When we closed, he said *Madame I didn't know*

You were racist, the way you denounced the Arabs

       And the role of whites. I was pregnant at the time.

He told me I should name my son, if the baby

       Was a boy, Martin Luther King. For me, then

Martin had been too pacifist. And still.

       Lumumba had been killed. Nonviolence

Betrayed. I found a way to say I would call

       My child what I wanted, my mind fixed

On the sovereignty of spices, how much pepper,

       Star anise, cinnamon and saffron, cassia and clove

Could alter the known worlds, what ships-full

       And demand for them would, in full time, spark

Colonization. What tales the Arab traders told

       To withhold the origins of their wares:

Wild winged creatures on cliff walls guarding

       Roosts built of cinnamon sticks, sightings

Of dragons, serpents, monstrous beasts,

       Furnished to the Romans and Greeks, to pique

Desire, to protect supplies, to lay the source

       Of a world economy with trade routes so

Fiercely fought over that new routes had

       To be found. What did the Director know

About all this or Martin Luther

       King of the Americas?

CRITIQUE DE LEÇONS

Exposé de la leçon:
  Madame reads the text with a nuanced and expressive
  voice; she invites a student to reread it; he deforms the
  vowels, neglecting euphonic liaisons, using a nasal and
  stressed accent. The professor corrects him both on
  reading errors and mispronunciations. The study of
  challenging vocabulary is done quickly and we move on
  to comprehension of the text. Madame strives to show
  to the students the concerns of the peasant and (as well
  as) his desires; she explains to them the literary images.
  All in the form of a conversation. An exercise of logical
  analysis closes the lesson. In summary: the explication
  was well-executed, the lesson aligns with the national
  program; that said, there should have been a certain pre-
  established and logical order in this *explication de texte*...

Pedagogical method and use of didactic material:
  Based on running dialogue between the class and
  Madame, the pedagogic method would be more effective
  if she had all the students participate in responding
  and if she wrote on the board the essential points of the
  lesson. It would also be necessary to control the activity
  of each student, his posture and behavior...

———————————————

Here is where I say Madame is my mother,
     that I am years from becoming both her and the
     administrator (veiled to the present but for his report
     which is a sort of short miracle, edges frayed now of
     onion-skin paper, frail and translucent as a layer of fog
                                                                lifting
on the March morning at the Athenée of Matadi,
1968). Hear a shuffling, the students taking their seats,
mindful that Madame has been joined by someone who
will appraise her, noting thirty students present, four
absent (why the missing we will never know: the river
not to be crossed, excuses brassy & imaginative). The
administrator will note Madame's inability *to control the
activity of each student, his posture and behavior*

                                                        and I will stand
(in the hall of my mind) (long after she is gone) in her
defense, balancing student-teacher ratios, considering
my mother: unforgivably conscientious (unforgivably
democratic such that her own children were not favored
above those of others). (How young and beautiful she
must have been, alive, teaching, tidy in a pale blouse and
pleated skirt, abundant hair piled into a beehive made
soft by the water of the air.)

Here we can hear the shuffling of my heart: the question
of why we were we not above all to her. (She will not be
able to answer it.) (She will never be able to answer it.)

Here I return to the story, which is hers and mine, and
the stories of mothers and children, the lessons of love
and knowledge, and unwitting neglect.

Here is where I say my mother was, in effect, orphaned as a child (which explains things but does not change them).

Here I will try to merge my love with a love that bursts open, thick as the Congo River, fraught as the glittering Atlantic.

A student of my own once told me *I did not make it to class because my throat closed*. That he had been painting with cadmium yellow. I did not believe him. Knowing nothing of cadmium yellow. That he could not breathe after painting with so much pigment (hue that makes the most muted and splendid sun) (color like no other) (how it can poison) (how other yellows will not do).

He returned to class alive.

What laboratories of transmission exist (in desire). How life pushes the throat open.

The administrator sits at the back of the room, observing, writing, observing, writing, observing, writing,

fly on the wall, full eye, peripheral, attuned to buzzings and movement, officially appointed to assess and account for (anointed to keep) the existing state of affairs (or shift them).

What he thinks of the lesson's heart he does not say.

His form holds no lines for addressing (by teachers or systems) the effects of violence, the legacies of colonial rule (or their undoings).

How Madame, my mother, arrived at the following text on the day of her assessment, I cannot say:
> *Vie de Paysan*, Life of the Peasant (B. Dadié).

How the sun broke through the classroom windows of the Athenée of Matadi, we cannot know.

How my mother relished a challenge.

What the students learned—and felt
> of the great Ivorian writer, B. Dadié,

Bernard Binlin Dadié, who speaks of love (praise), of Bernard Binlin Dadié né Koffi—to signal a Friday birth—Binlin to note "he who offers refreshment but drinks only water" (which is to say "the generous")—Dadié to carry the line,

to hold the tales told and retold,

to make tales refracting like the facets of gems.

> of the great Ivorian writer, B. Dadié,
> who writes:
Redis-moi en vers rythmés
. . .
Toute la geste africaine

Madame. Agent of refraction (praise). (My mother.)

Toute la geste africaine.
Toute la geste haitienne.
Toute la geste.

Dis moi

how the sun broke through the classroom windows
of the Athenée of Matadi

what it means to be open-throated

(what sensation of freedom. what technique to
promote release. what approach to bypass tension)

what it means to be like the yellow trumpet,
blossom of Congo, ample leaves lying low to the
ground, flower opening once and quickly dying,
followed by another flower

to be like the lemon tree, symbol of fidelity (sign of
luxury in the gardens of northern Europe)

to be the heady bud of the orange tree's flower:
azahra

the golden apple, a form of sun

light of sight.

Huitzilopochtli, before the time of the Americas,
required the human heart and human blood
(and so was fed the human heart and human blood)

(what sacrifices, and who the sacrificed)
for the sun to shine, for the universe
to hold.

Whose universe? Which universe?

How I turn to myth as milk (Isis, praise),
(headdress bearing a sun-disk)
model capable of elucidating life's
sticky contradictions,
narrative to decipher
this

narrative.

How we settle our truths
(confrontation)
(compromise)
(conciliation)

and fall back down to earth

(blood in our veins).

Reborn.

Here is my heart

or is it my mind?

Blood running red,
           coursing through my body,

                blood running black,

                           coursing through my body.

I have made no (other) bodies with my body.

I have instructed thousands of students in my years
as my mother, as myself,

fed them the milk of hours, broken open with them the
eggs of sundisks and struggle, what horns on the heads of
knowledge, wrestled down, what time forwarded, what time
thwarted to fill the blue lakes of lacunae, to add to existing
color.

In physics: Black is the famine
of color.
In art: Black is the harvest
of all colors.
                Add black.
                Add yellow in its metallic incarnation.
                Add black in its infinite quantity.
                Add black.

Add the dialogics of forward into time with neck
curved back.
Add the amniotic fluid of verse. The umbilical of the text.

The pedagogy of the pregnant silence.
The pedagogy of the open throat.

Learner. Apprentice. Praise.

Praise the blood running red, pulsing through the body.
The blood running black, pulsing through the body.

Blood of both beginnings and endings.
Blood of flows.

Blood of the Black body.

Black of the ultra mind.

There is a prayer in a poem of Dadié's:

Thank you God, for having made me Black,
I carry the World since the dawn of time
And my laughter on the World,
        at night
        creates the day.

It sits at the center of *this* book, and for you.

THE CONTRACT OF GEORGES, RODNEY

= G.B./JA. =

-REPUBLIQUE DEMOCRATIQUE DU CONGO.-

GOUVERNEMENT CENTRAL

MINISTÈRE DE L'ÉDUCATION NATIONALE.

-=-=-=-=-=-=-=-=-=-=-=-=-=-=-=-=-=-=

-ADMINISTRATION GENERALE.-

-=-=-=-=-=-=

1ère Direction

3ème Section.-

COMMISSION DE MISE EN PLACE N° EDN/DAG/813/1/105/03600
     DU 16/09/67

Monsieur   GEORGES Rodney

Matricule N°   31.117

Diplôme   INGENIEUR

Grade   REGENT

Spécialité   MATHEMATIQUES, PHYSIQUE et CHIMIE

est mis à la disposition de Monsieur le Directeur de l'Enseignment
             de la Province de KONGO CENTRAL (ATHENEE
             DE MOANDA)

pour être affecté dans une des Ecoles de son ressort pour l'année
             scolaire
             1967. . ./1968 . . . et 1968 / 1969

Dernière affectation
             INONGO

Kinshasa, le 15 septembre 1967.-

Pour le Directeur Chef de Service
de l'Administration Générale:
Le S/ DIRECTEUR-CHEF DE SECTION,

1 ex.   F.P. (Pers.Ens.Etranger)
1 ex.   B.C.T.
1 ex.   Intéressé
1 ex.   Province
1 ex.   Dossier

                                                  I am looking
Down the tunnel of time at a crusty document. I am typing
Toward the accessible map of Moanda. Toward the Athenée
Of Moanda. I am trying to solve for X. What I would like
To do is lower myself into the head of GEORGES, Rodney
And enter his eyes, but he is held down by the gentle sleep
Of the dead, so far gone when I travel to Congo fully formed.

The contract of GEORGES, Rodney points us to Moanda,
(Also Muanda, both pronunciations will get you to the same
Place), town and territory on the coast of the Atlantic
Where GEORGES, Rodney may have looked west into
A briny horizon and imagined his country at the edge
Of the waves some 6,000 miles away. There he must have
Heard a rush at the mouth of the Congo River—the deepest
In the world, more profound than the possibility of light
In zones. There he may have felt the rumbling of the river's
Deposits of clay, sand, silt, all its sediment and power
Into the Sea—and thought what?

67

I did not visit Moanda (I had yet to read his agreement
To remain there trading knowledge for knowledge, facts
For the flow of blood). We stayed in Kinshasa, then drove
To see the bonobos, our cousins who came down from
Their hills and trees when the guardian called out *Venez!*,
Accustomed to their jobs of self-presentation, of gesturing
I want (what is thrown over an electrified fence onto the
Waiting ground, onto their green gated fields, protection
And imprisonment).

There was much I wanted from that trip but could not temper:
The waterflow and Falls of Zongo composing their own meter
And rhyme, the sound of unstoppable time. I could not bribe
The water. I could not dam it.

Above us, an ibis kept tagging the sky, black-tipped wings wide,
Naked dark head low. A drone followed. Such forms as could
Take the wind did, and blew north to Zongo II Hydroelectric
Power Station, regulator of flow, carved in the bend of the Inkisi
River, daughter of the mighty Congo.

O Congo River, that flows to Moanda, mouth of the sea,
What have you to tell me now?

AN ACCOLADE AND ACHE

an accolade and ache accompany the quest for the missing
who are underscored arbitrarily and assigned axes and
agraffes here. what ablaze, afterglowing and ateliers in
the dormant archives. corners of amens, asterisks, aspects
of attention. *Ade.* _____. *Agenor. Alfred. Altenor.*
what assignations and alibis to arrive already avant-garde.
Antoine. Auguste. such backing into surnames. an assemblage
of back matter and bestrewings. what bridges spanned.
_____. *Backer. Bayard.* and bioluminescent flares from
burial beds. *Barberousse.* what bêtes noires you were to
the bête noire. *Bellerive.* how brave. *Bernard.* _____.
Blaise. _____. such birds of passage, appellations in
the eaves of basilica. *Blain. Bony.* _____. *Brizard.*
Bristou. in contiguity, in constancy. *Cantave.* cadre of a
series of calculations. *Chapoteau. Charles.* senders of cables,
dot after dot. *Carty. Champagne.* _____. *Chatelain.*
Condé. coding certitude and contention. *Corvenson.* en
double exemplaire. with delicacy explaining: I must depart.
Dambreville. with doubt and dream balanced. *Dartigue.*

Debrosse. _____. *Désil*. dogged. *Dormeus*. _____.
Durand. *Dussek̦*. echo of the first self. what elisions. *Elizé*.
Étienne. and fear as fire and phantom. *Faublas*. and fear
insufficient in form. *Fils-Aimé*. *Féthière*. *Fontaine*.
_____. *Ford*. *Fougère*. what freedom and unfurlings.
faculty and factotum of a new grappling. _____.
François. grapes of a next vine. *Georges*. *Gentil*. *Gilbert*.
_____. *Gouthier*. grasslands and thickets. which new
graphs spread over the ancient. _____. what questions of
justice. _____. *Jean-Noël*. _____. *Jocelyn*. *Jolibois*.
Joseph. *Kavanagh*. *Labbé*. _____. what loves lost. loves
followed. *Labbé*. *Lafond*. *Lamarque*. _____. *Lamour*.
the unrelenting ligatures. and leaves of impossible length.
Laurent. _____. *Lerebours*. such long shots. and
longings. _____. *Lescouflair*. *Louis*. with the making
of ways out of none. *Malan*. *Manigat*. _____. *Marcellus*.
McGuffy. by means of middle-men. *Milord*. _____.
with adamant memory. with mentions of a momentary mecca.
the alma mater. the middle passage.

Michaud. _____. *Moïse*. what new masters? *Mombleur-Jocelyn*. what maintenance of necessary futures. *Nerestant*. *Nicolas*. and not without naiveté. and without naiveté. _____. *Noël*. *Noisin*. what obligations and othersides. otherwises and ouvertures. *Osias*. how quiet partings. how profound. *Peck*. *Pickering*. _____. *Pierre*. *Pierre-Louis*. how pebbled and foot-held the path. _____. *Pratt*. _____. *Préval*. what references to la personne even through a punctuated distance. _____. which qualifications to present. _____. what answers to. what quid pro quo. and quotas. which panoramas. *Rémy*. *Romain*. what racings. and rates of exchange. and remittances. how hard the rain in seasons of rain. *Roy*. _____. *Roc*. what realignments and their reasons. what rebellions. what treasons. when the signs rotate in several senses. _____. who the resolved signatories. *Sanon*. *Sixto*. *St. Fort*. _____. *Sylvain*. through the savanna's scattered and widely spaced trees. *Sylvestre*. on the black tarmac. *Talleyrand*. *Tozin*. *Toussaint*. _____. *Vieux*. _____. *Wilson*. *Zéphirin*. on the flights. all kin and xeno and xangô.

CONGO—1965-1975

BECAUSE

joy can find its name
in many books

because joy can be
as rotund
as a baobab tree

THE ENVIRONMENT WAS DIFFERENT
FROM WHAT I HAD KNOWN ALL MY LIFE

in Haiti. The plants, the birds, the forest
animals I didn't see but heard giving
voice to the night.

I was sent to Kenge, a village in the middle
of the bush. Fresh food was hard to get.
No greens. No fowl.

No fish. Goat meat, none of that. I used
what I had. *Makondo*, plantains long
as two feet. *Saka saka*,

a kind of legume. Antelope, boar. I set aside
snake and larvae. Dinner was mostly
white rice, *saka*,

dry cod. Sardines sometimes, rehydrated
in salt baths, little silver bullets
with wide eyes.

cresson, bright green turning olive in the bouillon's stern heat.
meat from the pincers of red crab kissed by legume. bright
from the sea, all manner of fish with their milk-white bones.
culled from the bay, the pink ears of conch wrested from their
shells and boiled to forever. grilled too the conch and roasted
the corn 'til the kernels yellow-black call out *am I not yours?
am I not earnest?* from the hills, frilly lettuce, mirliton, ripe
tomatoes and apricots of the plots and brown hills embracing
the city. port-au-prince. the rice and callaloo, the gumbo,
the chaka mayi, griyo with pikliz, cabbage and carrots, hot
pepper and clear onion. descending on the road came the
ladies balancing such loads, hips calibrating the weight on
their heads. left. right. minds on their risks and futures and
sour and sweet things. and the desserts, blan manje, such
condensation of milk required, such coconut flesh, and gelatin.
vanilla and nutmeg. bread from all the bakeries, and all the
african stems and roots, and french adaptations, and native
fruit in a time of plenty and cease-fire.

WHAT WE FOUND NEW AND GLORIOUS

the heat in double measure of the pili pili, orange-red pepper
sauce sitting pretty atop the fufu, also doubly anointed, cassava
massaged to ball, pale and plump, polite companion of the
peanut stew in which all good things commune: ô chicken
and yam, rose tomato and white onion, coriander. sentinel of
the plantain, so sweetly fried, also yellow & sturdy with fish
dried and reborn next to beds of deep green mpondu leaves.
and glistening in its sweating bottle, the amber beer, like a
fresh baptism of the afternoon. who will deny liboké emerging
from a chartreuse sheath of banana fronds to puncture the air
with its surprise of impeccable spice. from the interior and
the lakes. from the coast. from the trees and through the roots
in the earth. transported by truck and by foot. transported
by women. the sustenance. the sweetness of caakiri's mix of
couscous and thick milk, yogurt, pineapple and tang. the
joining and eating by hand, and with fork and knife and
spoon. the moon meeting the day's light and covering the
gathered with pleasure.

AVENUE DES FLAMBOYANTS

The most sunsets I saw were in Kinshasa,
where we had many friends, where we

were happy and the sky, vast & singed
red, held up the sun until *en fin* they

gave up on Avenue des Flamboyants.
The trees fervent with crimson flowers

in the Belgian quarter and lights of Kinshasa.
We walked to church on gray-blue Sunday

mornings, past the market's jade closed
windows, to a mass whose bells chimed

our troubles, our future transcendence.
The god there was our god—alive

as we were, alive and antediluvian,
celadon sea, flaming suns behind us.

BEER AND BABIES

There was no television.

It was hot. What else was there
                 to do after work?

The men always talking politics.

The ocean crossed
                 —with children.

The fires of the world.

We were making new lives.

We were making a way in new towns.

A way by new rivers.

A way in our jobs.

A way with new sisters.

And ourselves.

A way.

IN KINSHASA

In our last year we were a good size group.

We formed organizations.

We had matches: football, volleyball.

We went to church.

We went to the movies.

BECAUSE

empire will make trouble
for your country

TROUBLE IN YOUR COUNTRY

The poor lived in the *cités*. Like Cité Soleil.
The personnel who came to you. To work

in your house. They used French and their
language. The difference between them

and the poor of Haiti is that the Zairois
poor were not illiterate and the Haitian

poor were. The *boy* had his newspaper
and came to our house and read to me

from it. He said *Madame Chapoteau:*
There is trouble in your country.

MAKAK

The men are called *boys*, and the women *mamas*
in the houses of the colony's former masters
on the land of the boys and mamas.

The whites are called *masters* and the natives
makak, and even with each other
they say *makak*.

And we say *makak* too at the smallest infraction
at the least mistake in the land of the boys
and the mamas.

The men enter the white houses to cook
and clean, the women to watch over
the babies by day.

The mambas glide through impossible grasses,
climb up the tallest trees. The makaks
are themselves

not knowing they're insults, moving swiftly
from tree to tree. They screech
in the night.

Of makaks and mamas and masters and boys
we can say this: a makak and *boy*
will become a man who becomes

a leopard who plays master, then is master
and the houses burn, and the fields
blow to ashes.

And the ashes, they whisper *makak*.

MOBUTU SESE SEKO, MESSIAH

To be neither left nor right, nor even center
but next to the ear of the martyr
divining

his end. To melt the body. To rise like
a god, hands clean of blood, mouth
open and full.

To utter *plenitude of power, warrior*
who goes from conquest to conquest,
leaving fire

in his wake. To observe the tall game.
To loom above the board.
To play it

casting an arm across a vastness
of territory. To rechristen
the cities.

To renounce the savagery of a king.
To announce a new
ferocity.

To be neither left nor right, nor even center
but next to your ear divining
your exit.

THE RECORD OF AN ATTEMPT TO PURGE THE COUNTRY OF COLONIAL INFLUENCE BY MOBUTU

(AND UNRELATEDLY A LIST OF CITIES IN WHICH HAITIANS LIVED, WITH UNDERSCORES SIGNALING ANTECEDENTS UNKNOWN TO ME)

What was _____   and was Léopoldville
                      became and is Kinshasa

What was _____   and was Élisabethville
                      became and is Lubumbashi

What was Kisangani   and was Stanleyville
                      re-became and is Kisangani

What was Lodja   and was Lodja remains Lodja
in what was _____   and was Kasaï-Oriental province
                      and is Sankuru province

What was _____   and was Bakwanga
                      became and is Mbuji-Mayi

What was Ngoma   and was Goma
                      remains Goma

What was _____   and was Baudouinville
                      and Virunga
                      became and is Moba

What was 'bu 'nkafu   and was Costermansville
                      and Costermansstad
                      became and is Bukavu

What was _____	and was Albertville became and is Kalemie
What was Kenge	and was Kenge remains Kenge
What was _____	and was Tshikapa remains Tshikapa
What was _____	and was Banningville became and is Bandundu
What was _____	and was Luluabourg became and is Kananga
What was _____	and was Thysville became and is Mbanza-Ngungu
What was Moanda	and was Moanda remains Moanda also Muanda
What was Matadi	and was Matadi remains Matadi

I COULD HAVE

spent my life there

A tall tree.
A vast grassland.
Swollen clouds that fill
A stretch of sky.
The pale horizon.
An antelope herd unsurprised
And grazing. The picture taker
Far and stiller than the faunae:
Long-legged on large hooves,
Frozen in their antelope affairs.
The tree humming soundlessly.
The clouds moving forever nowhere.

———————————

Kinshasa, 4 January 1969

Dear Mother,

I could not write you before. It's been 4 months
since I've been paid. Things are going better now.
We're working to set ourselves up in the USA.
You'll be with us in August. I am wishing you
a good and happy '69.

À bientôt,

R.

Everyone is doing well. Please send me information
on passport updates in Haiti. Mine has been cancelled.

Kinshasa, 1 June 1969

YOUR FOOTPRINTS

Hello Daco,

You must think that we forgot or are neglecting you,
which is not at all true, you are always in our thoughts.

For Mother's Day, if you didn't receive our letters as usual,
it's because we wanted to surprise you. This did not work

out. There remains barely one month and a half before we
will be with you. Rest so that you won't be too tired

for the long voyage to the States. In your next letter, send me
your footprints. I will buy you shoes on my passage through

Europe. I know you're getting ready little by little. Don't buy
any hats, especially. One doesn't wear hats there.

Nous t'embrassons. Porte toi bien.

Edmonde

CROSSINGS—1970s

THE TINTIN BOOKS

Who does not love Tintin, boy reporter, not knowing
I too am the native coming with the saw to saw off

the tail of Milou, the talking dog, en route to the Congo.
Who dives into the water off the ship on those watercolor

pages, the jade-blue. Next page, I am in the crowd of natives,
wearing one boot and one shoe by the rickety railroad.

To greet the great Tintin. A boy. A god. I am Tintin boy
god. Who takes on the roaring lion, who takes on a tribe

of Africans, who vanquishes the evil medicine man.
Returning triumphant. Pith helmet. Uniform of khakis.

The pages almost turn themselves. Tintin, boy reporter
on assignment. What is the lesson? What is the lesson?

And what is the lesson in Creole where *tintin* means
junk?

SUNDAY

We must have known
our parents delivered us
here so they could return
to Zaire, except maybe
Stephane, who was too small
to know anything but love.

We are a passel, a clump
of cousins at Tante Laurette's,
our round heads, braids decked
with ribbons, beady stares,
all seated by the concrete pool
when our photo is taken, well-fed
and serious as lizards in the sun.

UNWRITTEN LETTERS TO THEIR PARENTS BY CHILDREN BOARDING WITH RELATIVES IN PORT-AU-PRINCE

return, though we are safe and schooled
return, powdered with love
return, though precariously
return, though our passel of cousins love us
return, though we love them
return with mother's milk and father's milk
return as the day turns clear,
the afternoon rains over
the clouds like ships
the red school uniforms
return with more books from abroad
with *feux d'artifice,* stars so close to the earth
in the night's blue smoke
return with the pink meat of almonds
with the butter of dawn
with the afternoon mail

CROSSINGS—1986

POWER

I was away
at school

when my mother called.
Duvalier ale!

She was pacing forth
and back

I suspect. *Turn on
the TV* she yelled.

So I did. And there
was the scene,

a car moving
through the dark,

and through
the glinting

windshield:
Jean-Claude,

and Michèle
bearing a cigarette

in her left hand
over a bent and

supple wrist. Or
is it an insouciant

wrist. Or a melo-
dramatic wrist

sending fuck you
to the cameras

to the crowds
jeering

fuck you too. Or
is it a wrist

to fend off fear
with a capital

F, the panic
of what the fuck

is happening
here, the dread

of a figurative cliff
after which

the car
will spin, will

plunge,
the precipice

of the world
they have known

and ridden
ending.

In the back seat:
the baby and the body-

guard or a General
or someone.

Perhaps they know
nothing.

Perhaps they know
everything.

Guileless. Guilty
at once.

The child knows
wordlessly

the speed of the car
the what he has been

born to.
Not yet.

Jean-Claude
grips the wheel

with his hands
of death.

His job is to drive.
To *just drive*.

An American plane
awaits them.

It is always
an American

plane. To take them
from the heat

of their making.
Of the Americans'

making. A cigarette
burns in the closed

car. Outside:
the purple pre-dawn.

Gone: the furs and tropical
fridges for them.

Gone: the electricity
for green aquariums.

Gone: the golden gowns,
the turbans.

The flight
from Port-au-Prince

to Paris. The water
beading on the plane

window. The water
being swept away

by the wind.

CROSSINGS—ARTIFACTS

CARVED IVORY HEAD OF A WOMAN

taken from my mother's house many
years ago, whose provenance is the tusk
of a beast—whose fierce intelligence is
expressed in its amber eyes, whose flesh
is gray as a Lake Kivu dawn, whose memory
is long, whose eye is the size of a human's

—mine, fixed upon the study's top shelf
atop which sits the object—whose flesh
is the beige of bone, whose eyes are inversions,
whose visage is a sister's, by which I mean
a Black woman's, whose lips are beauty,
whose nostrils are a slight flare, whose coiffure
is the precise separation and togetherness
of cornrows, whose forehead is high

—whose origin resides in the sculptor's
mind's eye, in the concatenation of the model's
exquisite genes, whose father is a full moon,
whose mother is the sun—as all life is anointed,
and all life comes down—and the sound of the first
wound is made—as perfection is subtraction—
as a tusk is extracted—as the chisel bears down,
and the artifact formed and beheld,
as the right price conceived, and the sale
made with sweet words, and the item packed
and carried across land and air.

A CONGOLESE COTTON SHIRT EMBELLISHED WITH A PORTRAIT OF MOBUTU FROM THE COLLECTION OF THE TROPENMUSEUM IN AMSTERDAM

Your portrait sits atop a cotton field of black,
Of spikes, of gold & blood red,
L'homme du 24 Novembre

Banner blazing above your head. A somber tomb
This shirt, grave as your mien,
Grave as your '65

Surprise coup. Who knows more than you? Who
Vanquishes his enemies more
Than you?

Become a shirt now to be worn by a man whose
Beating heart will enliven your face.
You beat, beat.

The Belgians could not fix you. The Americans
Were your friends. You played them
You thought.

But the Dutch have you locked in a case. Museum
Capture. Praise shirt. God shirt from which you
Gaze out onto the world.

The body of Patrice Lumumba was dissolved in acid by his killers after his assassination in 1961. A tooth, all that remained, was transported to Belgium shortly thereafter. It was returned to Congo in June of 2022.

A CLOSING

Let it be planted near the violet starcluster
Whose flower is a symbol of the expanding world.

Let it be like the fruit of corn, manifestation
Of the sun, utterance of humanity.

Let it be a dark planet, sentinel and satellite, tutor
Of night, guardian of light.

CODA: CROSSINGS—2000s

BECAUSE

kin, xeno, xangô

CROSSINGS

I had no mother. I had no father.
I had a need tied to a cord
by a ball of flame. I ran.

When the running could sear no more,
when the horse of my body
stopped, I walked.

Nights of unspeakable stars. Shook
nature of my blood through
green reeds

of a river bottom. Plumes into silty ink.
Still, how cells will call to cells—
ancestor to the current.

> *I move through you.*
> *I move through you.*

————

There is only forward. That thing
at your back—you already know:

door and *don't,* gully, catacomb,
effluvium. *Ann ale!* Onward,

defying the blinding portal.
How sweet could be this bed

of mud, this rest of marrow,
bone, if one said—*no*.

————

Weight on the head. Weight on the back.
Arms of everything. Passels and rope.
Burden of freedom. Burnings.
Weight on the head. Weight on the back.

————

My cousin said: *come*
My husband said: *come*

————

The plantation owners said: *come*
The factory bosses said:
come

————

They said you'll find Life.
As if Life were a person you'd meet
on the street, a set of keys clinking against
a back pocket. As if Life were a god returned
from a bath, pulling blinds up to whisper
the names of three countries. *The wind
erases all borders.*

————

I crossed a line.
I crossed a line and disappeared.

————

Became no one. Belonged
to no country. Displaced
still I
saw—
by rectangles of rear-
views (eyes, nose, mouth even),
on ammonia-cleared floors, in windows
of nocturne's blackness
—myself.

————

What rights I had, I kept
in my head.   The right to—
                   The right to—
                   The right to—

wipe mirrors immaculate.
make the bed
but not lie in it. smooth
everything (divan, duvet's white down)
dissolve.

scatter.

————

I restyle myself
on the street. In the wagon-
back. In the dim. In the pinprick of light.
In the highway's rumble underfoot.
Through the floorboards.
Through the tires
pitching North.
Through the stiff-necked smoke.
By the smeared fist.
Through the stink of it all.

————

54 migrants in the back of a truck
women
men
children (one
with no mother, no father, no people)
no papers, no…
no… no… no…

————

I am restyled cooking.
I am remade eating, seated
on concrete, styrofoam
containers stacked.

————

I am con-
tained. I am
delayed.

———————

moving through you, I am
moving through you, I am

My body
become the border

My body
become the border
patrolled

My body
become the border
policed

———————

moving through you, I am
moving through you, I am

reborn dreaming,
attaining *flight*, sight
of my kin on the sea's other side,
their altars to adorn, their faces to adore,
which verse to verse in libation, how many
hurricanes make a new season,
how many carve the eye of ascension.

———————

The gap.

The Darién Gap,

ligature of Colombia and Panama,

site of South and Central encounter,

precursor.

Mapless

jungle.

America.

America.

Your soaring canopy.

————

What falls from the trees falls first from the sky.
Some say a curse spreads the day we arrive.

————

we slip—
we regain—
we stumble—
we remain—

Steadfast, some move fast—some move hard: launching
prayers to the masters of the winds, trading secrets with the
rock of small streams, admonishing the architects of the visible
and unseen worlds. some stand grammatically correct in their
claims—some with tongues of wrecks, slashing the syntax of
subtlety. Some do not speak. Some sing.

————

Nights of nothing
but rain.
Steam of pre-
dawns.
Fog of green
dawn.

————

Provisions lasting only so long.
The mind's provisions.
The visions of schools, of supermarkets gates
with their mechanical eyes, with cool-cool air,
with rows of a person's repair. Open.

————

They said: *Don't come.*
There is nothing for you here.
They said: *Let me be clear.*

————

The animal self.
What the eyes see.
A buzzing in the head.

Ask the coyote: *what is the most dangerous animal in these trees?*

He replies: *the mosquito.*

————

Are we insects?
Are we swarm?
Are we compound eyes, one pair of antennae?
Are we numbers in the jungle line?

————

—crossing Ecuador—crossing Peru—crossing Colombia and
Panama—Costa Rica—crossing Nicaragua—Honduras—
crossing Guatemala—crossing Mexico—*most of the Haitians
here have crossed ten countries*

to glimpse the southern border of the state of abundance

————

*crossed the jungle line / the jungle line / fresh horses and two-faced
gods / the fires of the former cités / the first grounds / coffee grinds
/ signals of satellites in leaves / gusts carrying green news / clouds
past the canopy / contradictions / confirmations / rumors of respite
/ newborns steaming from their mothers' worlds / gods in whose
blood arrows are dipped*

move with you—

————

The travel is done—
walking.

The travel is done—
by busload.

The travel is done—
by air.

———————

Who does it?
Who can do it?
Who walks?
Who swims?
Who sees the Rio Grande?

———————

Who fords the river and lives?
Who sees their children stretch
        like the limbs of deep-rooted trees?

Who hurries the horsemen
to the river's edge?

———————

The river's edge a razor
The river's edge an azure gleam
The horizon's split of water and sky
What hells and gods live in that line?

NOTES

"My beloved companion,": Italicized portions drawn from Patrice Lumumba's last letter to his wife, Pauline Opanga Lumumba, translated from the French by Helen R. Lane in *Lumumba Speaks: The Speeches and Writings of Patrice Lumumba, 1958–1961*, ed. Jean Van Lierde (Boston: Little, Brown and Company, 1972).

"Le Congo, c'est moi": Italicized portions drawn from Tchicaya U Tam'si's long poem and book *Le Ventre* (Paris: Présence Africaine, 1964), translated from the French by Peter Thompson, in *The Belly* (New Orleans: Diálogos, 2021).

"Estimada amiga,": Fidel Castro's words, in italics, drawn from *The Prison Letters of Fidel Castro*, translated from the Spanish by Efraim Conte, Russell Cobb, Liliana Segura, and Joanne Wright (New York: Nation Books, 2007).

"Headwaters": Poem's second half drawn and slightly amended from a passage in "The Congo River, artery of the basin" on www.origin -congo.wwf-sites.org/congo_basin_at_a_glance/area/ecosystems /rivers.

"The Work": Italicized portions of last three stanzas drawn from Patrice Lumumba's speech at the Ceremony of the Proclamation of the Congo's independence, June 30, 1960, translated from the French by Thomas Schmidt.

ACKNOWLEDGMENTS

Grateful acknowledgment is made to the editors of the following journals, who first published versions of these poems:

"What Is Water?" in the Academy of American Poets' *Poem-a-Day*

"Fidel Wears No Hat" and "Estimada amiga," in *Consequence*

"Power" in *Harvard Review*

"When a book is a sentence" in *Ibbetson Street*

"Instructions in Times of Emergency," "The Lake Behind You," and "Makak" in *Jalada/Transition*

"The Reasons of Ertha Élysée Auguste" and "Critique de Leçons" in *MaComère*

"Carved Ivory Head of a Woman" in *The Montreal Poetry Prize Anthology 2022*

"My beloved companion," and "A Reply of Pauline Opango Lumumba" in *Obsidian*

"François Duvalier, Country Doctor" and "François Duvalier, Living God" in *Stand Magazine*

"Simone Duvalier" and "A Congolese Cotton Shirt Embellished with a Portrait of Mobutu from the Collection of the Tropenmuseum in Amsterdam" in *spoKe* 6

"Crossings" in *spoKe* 9

"Because" (1) and "in this poem do not use the word revolution" in *sx salon*

"Cobalt," "Hands are a matter," "Whites in Congo Flee by Ferry," and "Le Congo, c'est moi" in *Transition*

🔳 🔳 🔳

Grateful acknowledgment is made to Enzo Silon Surin and to Central Square Press, which published the chapbook *Letters from Congo* in which these poems appear: "I Pray the United Nations Bureau Will Forward This Card to My Brother Rodney Georges Who Is Currently in the Congo, Whose Address I Don't Know," "Headwaters," "Beer and Babies," "The Tintin Books," "Postcard | Front and Back," "Letter from Léo," and "Unwritten Letters to Their Parents by Children Boarding with Relatives in Port-au-Prince."

🔳 🔳 🔳

I am grateful to editors Kendahl Radcliffe, Jennifer Scott, and Anja Werner for publishing my essay "From Port-au-Prince to Kinshasa: A Haitian Journey from the Americas to Africa" in *Anywhere but Here: Black Intellectuals in the Atlantic World and Beyond* (University Press of Mississippi, 2015). The essay serves as the basis of this book's introduction.

🔳 🔳 🔳

I am grateful to the following individuals and their families who opened the doors of their experiences to me through generous interviews and the sharing of memories, documents, artifacts, and contacts: Ertha Élysée Auguste, Karl Auguste, Immacula Pierre-Louis Bernard, Aziza Brathwaite Bey, Rigobert Carty,

Charles Chapoteau, Maryse Chapoteau, Charles Dupuy, Claude François, Edith François, Edmonde Legros Georges, Gerard M. Georges, Georgette Legros, Jean Malan, Lilia Malan, Max Manigat, Denise Marcellus, Rodney Marcellus, Jean-Claude Martineau, Serge Martineau, Georges Moïse, Jacqueline Romain, LeClerc Sylvestre, and Rosette Sylvestre.

Thanks to my friends and colleagues who support art in amazing ways, some of whom responded to the first poems and ideas of this book: Aziza Brathwaite Bey, Karen Frostig, Prilly Sanville, Grace Cambridge, Dahlma Llanos-Figueroa, Patrick Étienne, Luther Henkel, Layron Long, Jean Guerly Pétion, Martha Collins, Mady Holzer, Kevin Gallagher, Holly Guran, Daniel Bouchard, Atibon Nazaire, Ernest Baroni (for so much so long ago), Zanset Yo, Mary Buchinger, Hilary Sallick, Anne Riesenberg, Indran Amirthanayagam, Tom Laughlin, and my Langston's Legacy workshop members: Gavin Moses, Florence Ladd, Patrick Sylvain, Joshua Bennett, and Andrea Bossi.

A number of organizations and institutions enabled me to conduct research, think, travel, and write. Lesley University provided faculty research grants and assistance in the way of the fantastic graduate assistants who supported the Haiti-Congo project: Tiffany Meadows, Julia McMillan, and Leah Vincent. A 2022 residency at the Massachusetts Museum of Contemporary Art (MASS MoCA) allowed me to finish the book's coda. A 2013 Black Metropolis Research Consortium Fellowship (at the University of Chicago) supported the work, as did grants from the Massachusetts Cultural Council in 2014 and 2022. I am grateful, too, to the academic conferences that allowed me to share the work in progress, including the Transatlantic Studies Association, 2015; and the Caribbean Studies Association, 2009.

To Helene Atwan and Catherine Tung, who facilitated the emergence of this book: I can't thank you enough.

BIBLIOGRAPHY

Abi-Saab, Georges. *The United Nations Operation in the Congo, 1960–1964.* Oxford: Oxford University Press, 1978.

Buchanan, S. H. "Language and Identity: Haitians in New York City." *International Migration Review* 13, no. 2 (1979): 298–313.

Castro, Fidel. *The Prison Letters of Fidel Castro.* Translated from the Spanish by Efraim Conte, Russell Cobb, Liliana Segura, and Joanne Wright. New York: Nation Books, 2007.

Chamberlin, Waldo, Thomas Hovet Jr., and Erica Hovet. *A Chronology and Fact Book of the United Nations, 1941–1969.* Dobbs Ferry, NY: Oceano Publications, 1970.

De Witte, Ludo. *L'assassinat de Lumumba.* Paris: Éditions Karthala, 2000.

Eggers, Nicole, et al. *The United Nations and Decolonization.* New York: Routledge, 2020.

Fontaine, Pierre-Michel. "Haitian Immigrants in Boston: A Commentary." *Caribbean Immigration to the United States*, eds. Roy Bryce-Laport and Dolores M. Mortimer, 111–30. Washington, DC: Smithsonian Institution, 1983.

Fullerton, Garry. *UNESCO in the Congo.* Paris: United Nations Educational, Scientific and Cultural Organization, 1964.

Hochschild, Adam. *King Leopold's Ghost: A Story of Greed, Terror, and Heroism in Colonial Africa.* Boston: Houghton Mifflin, 1998.

Jackson, Regine O. "The Failure of Categories: Haitians in the United Nations Organization in the Congo, 1960–1964." *Journal of Haitian Studies* 20, no. 1 (2014): 34–64.

Joseph, Peniel. *Waiting 'Til the Midnight Hour: A Narrative History of Black Power in America*. New York: Holt Paperbacks, 2007.

Kelley, Robin, D. G. *Freedom Dreams: The Black Radical Imagination*. Boston: Beacon Press, 2003.

Khôi, Lê Thành, et al. *L'Enseignment en Afrique Tropical*. Paris: Press Universitaires de France, 1971.

Kuyu, Camille. *Les Haitiens au Congo*. Paris: L'Harmattan, 2006.

Luard, Evan. *A History of the United Nations*. Vol. 2, *The Age of Decolonization, 1955–1965*. New York: St. Martin's Press, 1982.

Lumumba, Patrice. *Lumumba Speaks: The Speeches and Writings of Patrice Lumumba, 1958–1961*. Translated from the French by Helen R. Lane. Edited by Jean Van Lierde. Boston: Little, Brown and Company, 1972.

Meditz, Sandra W., and Tim Merrill, eds. *Zaire: A Country Study*. Baton Rouge, LA: Claitors Publishing Division, 1995.

Message of President James Monroe at the Commencement of the First Session of the 18th Congress (The Monroe Doctrine), December 2, 1823; Presidential Messages of the 18th Congress, ca. December 2, 1823–ca. March 3, 1825; Record Group 46; Records of the United States Senate, 1789–1990. Washington, DC: National Archives.

Nicholls, David. *From Dessalines to Duvalier: Race, Colour, and National Independence in Haiti*. Rev. ed. New Brunswick, NJ: Rutgers University Press, 1996.

Nzongola-Ntalaja, Georges. *The Congo from Leopold to Kabila: A People's History*. London: Zed Books, 2002.

O'Balance, Edgar. *The Congo-Zaire Experience, 1960–98*. New York: MacMillan, 2000.

O'Brien, Conor Cruise. *To Katanga and Back: A UN Case History*. New York: Simon & Schuster, 1962.

Papers of Maurice Dartigue. https://atom.archives.unesco.org/papers-of-maurice-dartigue.

Peck, Raoul. *Lumumba: La mort du prophète*. Paris: Velvet Film, 1992.

Prendergast, John, and Fidel Bafilemba. *Congo Stories: Battling Five Centuries of Exploitation and Greed.* New York: Hachette Book Group, 2018.

Radcliffe, Kendahl, Jennifer Scott, and Anja Werner, eds. *Anywhere but Here: Black Intellectuals in the Atlantic World and Beyond.* Jackson: University Press of Mississippi, 2015.

Randall, Stephen, and Graeme Mount. *The Caribbean Basin: An International History.* London: Routledge, 1998.

Struelens, Michel. *The United Nations in the Congo, or O.N.U.C., and International Politics.* Brussels: Max Arnold, 1976.

Trouillot, Michel-Rolph. *Haiti, State Against Nation: The Origins and Legacy of Duvalierism.* New York: Monthly Review Press, 1990.

Ulysse, Gina. "Why Haiti Needs New Narratives Now More Than Ever." *Tectonic Shifts: Haiti Since the Earthquake,* ed. Mark Schuller and Pablo Morales, 240–45. Sterling, VA: Kumarian Press, 2012.

UNESCO. "UNESCO in Sub-Saharan Africa." *50 Years for Education.* 1998. http://www.unesco.org/education/educprog/50y/brochure.

US Department of State. "Background Note: Democratic Republic of the Congo." Modified April 30, 2012. http://www.state.gov/r/pa/ei/bgn/2823.htm,.

U Tam'si, Tchicaya. *The Belly.* Translated from the French by Peter Thompson. New Orleans: Diálogos Books, 2021.

Verna, Chantalle F. *Haiti and the Uses of America.* New Brunswick, NJ: Rutgers University Press, 2017.

INTERVIEWS

Bernard, Immacula Pierre-Louis. Interview by author, recorded, Boston, June 15, 2007.

Carty, Rigobert. Email messages to author from Miami, August 2008; interview by author, recorded, Boston, July 12, 2008.

Chapoteau, Charles. Interview by author, recorded, Port-au-Prince, August 11, 2010.

Chapoteau, Maryse. Interview by author, recorded, Port-au-Prince, August 11, 2010.

Georges, Edmonde. Interview by author, recorded, Miami, August 12, 2006.

Malan, Jean. Interview by author, recorded, Boston, July 17, 2006.

Malan, Lilia. Interview by author, recorded, Boston, July 17, 2006.

Manigat, Max. Email message to author, Miami, July 31, 2008.

Marcellus, Denise. Interview by author, recorded, Boston, October 21, 2011

Marcellus, Rodney. Interview by author, recorded, Boston, October 21, 2011

Martineau, Jean-Claude. Interview by author, recorded, Montreal, December 15, 2011.

Romain, Jacqueline. Interview by author, recorded, Quincy, Mass., August 17, 2011.

ADDITIONAL INTERVIEWS/CONVERSATIONS BETWEEN 2000 AND 2012

Auguste, Karl. Montreal.

Braithwaite Bey, Aziza. Boston.

Dupuy, Charles. Montreal.

Élysée Auguste, Ertha. Montreal.

François, Edith. Boston.

Georges, Gerard. Boston.

Legros, Georgette. Port-au-Prince.

Martineau, Serge. Port-au-Prince.

Moise, Georges. Boston.

Plaisimond, Marcus. Cambridge, Mass.

Sylvestre, LeClerc. Atlanta.

Sylvestre, Rosette. Atlanta.

ABOUT THE AUTHOR

Danielle Legros Georges is a Haitian-born, Boston-based poet, anthologist, scholar, and translator. From 2014 to 2019, she served as the poet laureate of Boston. She is professor emerita of creative writing at Lesley University. Her work has been supported by fellowships and grants from the American Antiquarian Society, the PEN/Heim Translation Fund, the Massachusetts Museum of Contemporary Art, the Massachusetts Cultural Council, the Boston Foundation, and the Black Metropolis Research Consortium.